While every precaution has been taken in the preparation of this book, the publisher assumes no responsibility for errors or omissions, or for damages resulting from the use of the information contained herein.

THE EXCLUSIVE MILLENNIAL BLUEPRINT

First edition. October 29, 2017.

Copyright © 2017 vanessa gowora.

ISBN: 979-8227098665

Written by vanessa gowora.

EXCLUSIVE MILLENNIAL BLUEPRINT

VANESSA GOWORA

Idea Behind This Book

My life story is pretty simple, I have spent the better part of my life trying to understand people and what separates those who are successful from the unsuccessful. It helped that I have been to ten schools including universities and lived in three continents. People are not as complicated as they make themselves out to be. There are guidelines to everything including success and what you need to do is find the link.

There are of course so many resources out there, podcasts, newspapers and blogs on successful people. What makes this book any different from the hoards of resources out there, firstly unless you scourge the internet with a toothpick it's hard to find information on people who are young. Sure there are some that stick out like Lewis Howes or Adam Braun, but that's because it took them ages for their names to be recognized. As millennials our perceptions are different.

They are the greats like Oprah Winfrey and Richard Branson, but it's hard to imagine yourself in their shoes, they have accomplished so much and the age gap separates us from them. I wrote this book because I was tired of reading articles on people who I couldn't relate to, I was fed up about going through the internet and not finding many young people out there. There are far more young people making a difference out there than meets the eye, they were far too many of them for me to write in this book.

In writing this book I found myself being inspired by the stories, I imagined myself being moved by them, but these stories made me realize how people become successful. It also made me realize how everyone's success story is different, most motivational books make you feel depressed because it feels as if there's a particular road map. If you're not following that road map then chances are you won't succeed. Then there are the books that make you want to scream because they talk about having enough experience and know-how to go out there.

Times have changed and so have expectations, we are required to have years of experience, to be a certain way or accomplish something specific to be considered for a job. Interviews are a nightmare because of the interviewers stern glances and our different perspectives.

I came across stories of young people going out there and making a difference, some started as young as twelve others in their early twenties. They came from all different backgrounds, some lived in undesirable neighborhoods, others had drugged out parents and many didn't have any experience at all. They had an idea.

That is what I came to realize what success is and it isn't about having years of experience under your belt or a bank account flowing with money. It isn't about spending years in a company only to realize you want more. Sure those people are successful in their own right, but like I said before times have changed.

The Grant Cardones, Tony Robbins and Tim Ferris don't appeal to the younger people because they achieved ultimate success in their forties. Not saying we shouldn't learn from them because we should, they have achieved a lot. Guidelines are critical to any person's success, they push you in the right direction and help you not to make the wrong decisions.

Just like our perception is different, the same if for those who come from different generations who see us a nuisance. What I have discovered about this generation is they value doing what they are passionate about, but that can be tricky if you are unsure how to go through with it. I used to think I needed to be great at technology to succeed, but that's a misconception. The success stories all range from people who believed that they weren't exactly good at anything.

Our backgrounds, culture, beliefs and circumstances may be different, but two things align us and that is wanting to make a difference and our passion. Regardless of what you are good at and what you can't, this generation wants to inspire people and change the world. It could be we are a generation that has more options, opportunities and passions that any other generation. It can also be the downturn of the economy when job security isn't how it used to be, or the fact that this generation feels more responsible for their actions. Whatever it is people are stepping out of the shadows and declaring that they want to help people.

So how should you use this book?

This book is a guideline, but more importantly it's an inspirational tale of twenty five people below the age of thirty five who decided they were tired of living by other people's standards. Use it to motivate you and maybe by reading this you can discover your passions and dreams in the process.

How did I choose who to include in this book?

It took months of research in finding the right candidates at the right ages. Which was no easy feat, they were sites that had young successful people, but most of it was outdated so the search continued and continued. I thought of putting Mark Zuckerberg at one point and I didn't because everyone knows his story. So I tried to write people that weren't as popular as Mark Zuckerberg. There are a few names you will recognize of course, but their stories inspired me so much that I had to put in this book. My list came up to 110 and it's still growing.

The second process was now reading their articles and researching about them, this also took time as there wasn't a lot of information out there. They were a lot of podcasts on them and as great as podcasts are, I feel sometimes that it doesn't hit the right notes at the right time, you have to repeat the podcast. I wanted a written version of the interview.

There were many people who I wanted to put in this book, but the unfortunate part was after spending so much time searching for information on them I couldn't. So I gave up the chase.

Adam Braun

Pencils of Promise

"Make your life a story worth telling."

Many of us haven't heard of Adam Braun and his incredible journey. Adam has achieved more in his three decades than people twice his age, there's no limit to what is possible when it comes to helping the world. That is what Adam strives for, to make the world a better place. He faced many obstacles to get to where he is today, but that didn't stop him from achieving immense success.

Like most people Adam Braun had a normal childhood, he was born to conservative Jewish parents in 1983, in Greenwich, Connecticut. When Adam graduated from High School he went on to play for the Basketball Varsity team at Browns University. Braun who was so curious about the world joined a program called Semester at Sea, he was so enamored with what he saw in the fifty different countries he visited that he wanted to understand the needs of the local kids. The one thing that stuck out at him was when he was in India and a boy begging on the streets wanted a pencil. It was a simple thing, after all he came from a developed country where everyone could get a pencil.

This encounter struck a chord and he was inspired to start an organization called Pencils of Promise.

After this point I'm probably sure if you didn't know who Adam Braun is you now know. When Braun was twenty five years old he went on a journey that would change the world, it was then that he founded the company that would change thousands of kids lives throughout the world. At the time Braun only had $25 dollars in his bank account, he used crowd sourcing for him to get funds to start the company. The company took off and four years later they founded over hundred schools all over the world. They have served 35, 000 children throughout the developing world as of now.

Adam Braun like every person pursuing something out of the norm went through a variety of challenges in order for him to get to this point. Most of them were personal challenges and some were due to his lack of finances in building a charitable organization. It's no small feat to take up a challenge of going beyond the building blocks set up by those who came before us to take the other route.

Adam did that. He was faced with the possibility that people would see him in a negative light even though he was doing charity work. He assumed people might in fact see as a person who was doing this as a facade just to get the limelight.

There's a misguided perception that once all our dreams come true or we are in the process of them fulfilling that challenges cease to exist. People who have made it have all stated that it's far more difficult to find harmony once success comes. How can we balance our old life with our new once we are corporate leaders? The problem lies with the discordance between the new and the old; the new friends and the old who propelled you to where you are. Your family who stood by your side and the family that came along with the business.

Adam had to maneuver his way around the new and the old, it took him a while, but it is a learning curve for all of us.

Often we say that in order to be successful you need to have money to fund the endeavor. It's a saying that has become more of an excuse as times are changing.

Maybe, in retrospect years ago it would have made sense, but times have changed.

I'm sure that's another saying that's an annoying tick that you can't get rid of, but it's true. Back when the world wide web was in its infancy, people had a hard time coming to grips with building their own companies. Most would work in the corporate industry until they got tired and wanted to follow their passion. Usually that happened when they hit the age of forty and above. Now, people as young as seventeen are millionaires. If you're thinking that it's just dumb luck or that they came from wealthy families and that explains it.

These seventeen year old kids only had an idea, a fragment of a vision and a deep rooted need to be more than just mediocre. That's it. Passion plus dedication plus determination equals results. For Adam it was his passion for making the world a better place. It was what kept him up at night, he needed to be part of something greater than himself. One idea of kid wanting a pencil started a frenzy of ideas that led to Adam wanting to build schools in developing countries. It took a Semester at Sea to look at the world from a different perspective, he saw the world through the eyes of others who didn't from a developing country.

What if he hadn't spent a Semester at Sea? Would he be where he is today? It's hard to tell, maybe he would have come up with something different from Pencils of Promise. What can be garnered from Adam's life journey is he went on a journey to find out what he really wanted. He worked in the corporate world for two years then he signed his resignation letter. He left with only $25 dollars in his bank account and started Pencils of Promise.

Lewis Howes

School of Greatness

"Some are born great, some achieve greatness and some have greatness thrust on them upon them." Shakespeare

The beginning of this year when I was going through emotional turmoil I came across Lewis Howes video series. Here was this ordinary guy teaching me how I could make a difference in my life and follow my dreams, I didn't end up watching all the videos in time before they were taken down. His advice struck a chord in me and then I did research on him and what I discovered compelled me to find out more. I subscribed to his blog, downloaded his podcast and read his book to find out who this guy really was.

Lewis Howes story is simple. He was born in an average American family to supportive parents and two older siblings. As a child, Lewis wanted to be great, more than that he craved it especially when he watched football with his father. He wanted to be an All-American football star, he didn't know how he would get there, what mattered to him was getting there. At school, he struggled to cope and felt like he was idiotic. A part of him broke every time his teachers called him out on it. When his older brother was sentenced to jail, it made his life a whole lot harder. The man who had been his idol was getting locked up because life at home was hard and for any eight year old kid that could easily send them down the creek.

Lewis had to be spent the better part of his childhood having people whisper about him and his family when he walked passed. This however isn't the typical story of a convict who keeps getting thrown back into prison when they are released. Christian Howes while behind bars was working on his music as a jazz musician. He put in the hours, time and dedication and was released for good behavior. What happened after that is Christian sought to be the best jazz musician and play alongside the greats and that he did. This in turn inspired Lewis to continue seeking greatness.

Greatness finally hit on his door when he went to Principia College and Capital University to play football. Lewis became an All-American football player. He became a NCAA record holder for the most receiving yards in a single game in a 2002 game against Martin Luther College. After college he played football for two years until he got seriously injured while playing. Lewis had snapped his wrist. The last game he went for corrective surgery and this in result ended his career.

At the time he was only twenty four years old and had to deal with the fact that his dream was slipping through his fingertips, he had believed football would make him great, but in a way it did. For a year, he slept on his sister's couch, wondering what was the next step for him, clearly he couldn't go back to football so instead he scoured the web for anything for him to do. He found a site called LinkedIn, back then it was in its early stages and Lewis saw an opportunity to offer networking skills for free.

Eventually he created a business around that, but still something just didn't feel right. He was a millionaire, speaking around the world and people were begging to interview a twenty something year old. Lewis had achieved greatness, but he wanted to impact the world further so he created a podcast called School of Greatness featuring top people in every industry who have achieved greatness.

In 2015, he released a book called The School of Greatness. Millions of people download his podcast and subscribe to his blog.

What you can learn from Lewis Howes is that your passion can literally change your life if you allow it. Growing up I loved the Shakespearean quote on greatness. Who honestly wouldn't want to be great, to live life on their terms and not work for someone who dictates how you should live it.

We all want to be great. Some are blessed to have been born with an athletic ability and there are those who weren't, but that doesn't take away your ability to manifest what you want. What Lewis and Adam have in common is they wanted to change the world. Adam wanted to do it with something as simple as a pencil, but to thousands of people it meant the chance to get an education. Lewis wanted more than anything to be great and show the world it was possible to be great and they all started this journey in their twenties.

The world has led us believe that being great has to be adorned on us like a crown or an esoteric quality few people will ever have. Take a look at Lewis and you can see a man who came from a low income family who lived on the wrong side of the tracks, he could have easily become a crook or gave up on life. He chose not to be. What we have are choices and options. Today you can choose to look at what's wrong in your life, whether you are overworked, living paycheck-to-paycheck and doing something you hate. You have a choice.

What I love about Lewis Howes's story is it isn't about a genius behind a computer, a child prodigy, the son of a millionaire or a celebrity. Sure, he played football, but had one of the shortest careers in football, but regardless of that he achieved greatness by looking at what he could provide as a service and delivering on that.

Ashley Zahabian

"I have never met a great leader who couldn't be an even better servant."
Ashley Zahabian

Ashley started younger than most, but her childhood hasn't exactly been the easiest. It's hard to tell considering where she is right now and what she has achieved. At twenty two years old she has traveled the world speaking to young people and is seen as the new generation of motivational speakers.

We all go through seasons of intense pain and this is harder to deal with at the age of fourteen and whilst most of us our cowering away, Ashley chose to fight. She was an overweight fourteen year old kid who refused to allow that to dictate what happens in her life so she focused on the positive and lost the weight. But it took her four years to come to grips with who she was and what she wanted to overcome, she was bullied and her insecurities only made her stronger. Ashley started to lose control of her life and the people around her didn't know anything about it, her parents were clueless that this was happening.

It's normal to compare ourselves to people and Ashley did exactly that. She would go to the gym and compare herself to others who had a better body, but the more she worked out, the more her mental state changed.

At first, all she wanted was to lose the weight, but working out not only changed her weight, the change manifested in her mind. Even though she was changing, she was admitted to the hospital because she fell ill and the doctor told her she was dying. At that point in her life she had to deal with a massive blow to her ego because she had thought she was being healthy.

Ashley just ignored the words, but after four years of bouncing from one hospital to the next, Ashley had enough. She willed herself to look inside her and face the pain, not a lot of people can do that, but Ashley did it. Ashley cut-off from the world had no access to gadgets and her parents weren't around so she had to look within herself and change. There were a lot of changes Ashley had to deal with and she had to isolate herself away from the world in order to immerse herself in personal growth. Once that happened, her insides started to shift and her outside changed as well. At twenty two years old, Ashley believes that life is fair, but people rarely see it because they are focused on the negativity, life gives you exactly what you deserve.

What she has gone through has gotten her a huge following and she continues to inspire young women to follow their dreams. Ashley does it all, voice-overs, speaking seminars, videos and she strives to be the person she was created to be. Uncensored, inspiring, truthful and vulnerable. This is to give people hope and share her story so people can learn from it.There's a lot you can learn from Ashley who dealt with pain at a very young age and decided that it wouldn't affect her anymore.

People deal with pain in different ways, they find ways to hide it or run away from it. Some fight it, but give up before the race is finished while others just ignore it.

Ashley's story is about fighting back. She's changing the world by proving to people how possible it is to change your life by looking within yourself and fighting back. If you ever have been powerless then you know how hard it is to be in a match between yourself. We often think the miserable, depressed and hurt part of ourselves is stronger than the part of ourselves that has had to endure the good and bad seasons.

Ashley isn't quite finished with what she wants to achieve, she wants to create an emotional intelligence university by twenty four or twenty five. She has even come up with the curriculum. Only time can tell what she will do next.

Believe In Yourself – Inspirational Speech by Ashley Zahabian – Transcript:

Why is it we don't believe in ourselves?

That as soon as things get tough in our lives we start doubting ourselves

We start thinking that we may not make it

Stressing, worrying, imagining things that *may* go wrong in the future

We need to understand, the human mind is the most powerful tool we own, but it can also be the most DESTRUCTIVE

And we need to learn how to take control of the direction of our mind and our emotions

Your mind is going to provide you with your greatest challenges in life, because it is so powerful

So, if you can conquer your mind, you can pretty much conquer anything else around you, literally.

When writing the story of your life – make sure YOU hold the pen

Make sure not only that you hold the pen, but you write the script from your heart. Be brave when writing your script, it's your story and there are NO LIMITS to what you can have, what you can do or what you can be.

How bad do you want it?

You have to prove it to yourself that you want it bad enough, it's gotta hurt you not to get it.

And that's when you're going to learn to conquer your mind. Your mind will no longer be able to say no, because your inner heart and mind are aligned, and now NOTHING can stop you!

It's easy to be all positive and consistent when everything is going your way

But that's not life, that's not realistic!

Are you going to be one of the very few to stand up when things are tough, when everything is going against you.

Will you be able to believe in what's right, and what brings results to your life.

THAT'S WHEN YOUR CHARACTER WILL SHINE!

THAT'S WHEN YOUR STORY WILL BE BORN!

YOUR story is valuable!

YOUR story of success!

You can't build a STORY if you stop now. If you give up.

The world is full of people who gave up.

THE WORLD NEEDS HOPE. WE ALL DO.

The world needs you to STAND UP – to fight through your challenging moments,

To SHINE through the dark times

To love through the hate, and to be the difference in an indifferent world.

To BELIVE IN YOURSELF

Most people are bloated with ordinary thoughts and mindsets

They're so full of average that they have no more appetite

But you have to have an appetite for EXTRAORDINARY

Beyond what people are doing – think beyond them

THERE WILL ALWAYS BE DOUBTERS, and people below you, and people trying to put you down so they can feel higher, but you gotta STAY TRUE TO YOURSELF.

BELIEVE in your mind. Have some tunnel vision.

Then one day you will have your moment.

Because ANYTHING is possible if you just BELIEVE!

FEED your DREAMS.

If you can suffer through setbacks, through pain, RISE up with resilience once again, and again, and again!

ONE DAY THIS WORLD WILL TAP YOU ON THE SHOULDER & say "This is your time to shine"

YOU CAN HAVE BE AND DO ANYTHING YOU WANT

You just have to believe

Pete Cashmore

Mashable

"Execution really shapes whether your company takes off or not." Pete Cashmore

What do Pete Cashmore and Mark Zuckerberg have in common? Pete Cashmore just like Mark Zuckerberg started companies at the age of nineteen around the theme of connecting the masses. Mashable has become the social media news blog that has become one of the most profitable websites in the world.

Majority of people in their twenties have heard of Mashable and the journey all started when Pete was just nineteen years old. Way back in 2003, a seventeen year old Pete wanted to jump on the bandwagon of Japanese gizmos that were weeping the UK and Pete who lived in rural Scotland was determined to become part of the frenzy.

Unfortunately for him or bad timing, he made a huge loss with physical products because of the shopping cost, tax and the consignments of large blasters. For most people this loss would have dampened their spirit, but Pete rose to the occasion and researched on ways to make money. That is when Mashable.com was born. Mashable almost didn't happen, Pete went through a number of hurdles for it to be made possible.

Every successful person has to go through many obstacles to reach the peak of the mountain or to get a taste of success. In 2005, Pete was admitted to the hospital for his appendix, there were complications during surgery and he was forced to spend time recuperating at home. The separation from his peers who were obsessing over school and from life outside his home compelled him to create a website to push away the boredom.

He did all the leg work necessary for him to start a blog and emerged the social media giants such as Youtube, Facebook and Myspace. Pete cleverly coined the word mash-ups and created Mashable from it, at the time it was an online trend. Sites were combining videos, music and photos from a variety of sites.

Cashmore had created the site has the building blocks to his next start-up, but to the readers it was a no nonsense tool to get the most out of social media and to showcase new technologies and gadgets. It took nine months after the site had launched for Pete to attract his first advertiser who wanted to sponsor the site for $3000.

What makes Mashable so different from hundreds of sites that do the same thing is it's lingo, people who are tech junkies will be invested in it and so will ordinary Johns who want to know more, but are unsure on how to start.

Cashmore achieved the impossible because in less than ten months Mashable was one of the top ten blogs. The operation relocated to San Francisco and this is where weblog Gawker labeled him "the planet's sexiest geek", he was also featured in an article titled "The Playboys of Tech", in the US Style bible Details.

Pete's life drastically changed after that, he was a subject of a documentary on Al Gore's cable channel and was given the moniker Brad Pitt of the Blogosphere. Pete even had a photographer who trailed him. To brand the company, Pete organized Mashable parties and events. In 2010, AOL wanted to buy Mashable, but Pete turned them down. TechCrunch, which was one of Mashable's biggest competitor had been bought out and was bought for $25 million.

Pete has come a long way from being the sick kid who spent his days holed up in his room. Mashable has over 12 million views and it's ever expanding. He writes for Mashable as a columnist for technology and for CNN as a social media columnist. There's no doubt that he has more plans under his sleeve, but we have to watch out to see what he does next.

Nathan Chan

Foundr

"We often look up to super successful entrepreneurs and think they're not human. Truth is, they're exactly the same as you or me." Nathan Chan

Print magazines and Newspapers have been declining in recent years, people now are more concerned with investing with digital magazines. That is what most people now are doing including Brad Cameron who created the digital magazine called Build Your Empire. Nathan's idea was the same thing, he was born in Australia and wanted to have a magazine targeted at novice entrepreneurs.

Great idea, right. The problem was Nathan wasn't well known and had no idea how to publicize his magazine. Nathan was working a full time job back then and also working on the magazine. He wanted to find ways to grow his magazine so used Instagram as the vessel to do exactly that. Though he wasn't primarily focused on it, he still managed to get about 500 followers and whilst he was promoting the magazine via his Instagram channel he saw that there was a boost in subscriptions. When he noticed this he started to develop an aggressive Instagram marketing campaign. Within the first months he had 100,000 followers and 500,000 followers a year and a half later.

Before Foundr, Nathan had no idea where to start from, he knew he wanted to ask questions to successful entrepreneurs, he wanted to create something for the young who were yet to start their own businesses as there was nothing like it out there. To him print was a dying trade and still is by the decline of people buying print magazines.

Creating Foundr was a side hustle to him and he knew it would be a lot of fun, he was also into marketing and that was when Foundr was born. It wasn't part of the plan that Foundr would service millions of people or that what Nathan was creating was a start-up. Nathan had done the leg-work before Foundr, he had gone back to university to study, he did his second degree in marketing that complimented his first degree in IT. He also did online marketing to enhance his skills.

It wasn't smooth sailing after that, the early days were just as hard as setting it up. They were sued in the first four months by a big trade company in the States, the magazine was called something else and they had to re-brand and cut off the E from Foundr. Though there's no magazine out there with a letter E in Foundr, Nathan wanted to cover his back by making sure no one could sue him again.

Nathan's objective was to ask questions on how to stand out from all those people in the world, he wanted to know how people could get their content read or their products consumed. Many people think that those who set up businesses have a clue what they are doing, but they don't. They struggle with questions of how to differentiate themselves, on how to market, what products to create and Nathan grappled with those questions too. What he did was take his time to figure things out and fine tune them. Along the way Nathan realized there's a lot of power to having a magazine and it also makes it easier to get in touch with people who other people struggle to get a hold of.

It was a learning curve for Nathan who had to quickly learn how to publish a magazine especially considering he had no experience in doing that. He had to have a polished magazine and service the paying customers waiting for the magazine at the end of the day. The first issue of the magazine had a stock image of someone with a Superman look on the front cover.

From the first issue Nathan realized there was so much he needed to learn, it wasn't only about how to create a magazine, but how the magazine would look and how to ship it every month. Most people would have given up and chosen not to follow through, but Nathan had to take time to think how to make things work. Two and a half years later they haven't missed a shipping order.

When they first started out it was only three people. Nathan had to do most of the writing, editing and proofreading. His friends helped with the writing and his mother would proofread.

Fast forward to 2017 and Foundr is one the top digital magazines, the likes of Richard Branson, Tony Robbins, Marie Forleo and Arianna Huffington have graced the cover of his magazine.

JOEL BROWN

Addicted2Success

"You can't just wish for a better life, you must go out there and create it."

Joel Brown

Joel Brown has done a lot of great things in his life and he's only twenty nine. At the age of thirteen he knew he wanted more, he was passionate about music, production and being a DJ. So what did he do that most thirteen year old kids wouldn't dare do, he started to network with local radio stations in Perth, Australia. The radio shows refused, but that didn't mean Joel gave up on producing one of the shows. Finally after they got tired of his nagging, they gave up and allowed him to produce one of their shows.

At the age of fifteen he had his own radio show, it was there that he learned the art of platform making. Joel had gotten a taste of how it felt to be a part of the music industry, he worked alongside one of the best DJ's in Australia and pitched his music. The music landed in the hands of Grammy Award winning multi-platinum producer Jim Jonsin who has worked with Lollipop, T.I, Beyonce and Lil Wayne. Joel got the opportunity to go to Miami and work alongside with a lot of successful musicians. Joel was still a teenager who was talking to people who were twice his age and in the process of it all he learned how to apply himself and if you prove yourself, people will listen.

Joel had done the near impossible, by immersing himself in the music industry as a manager at a young age. For a few years, he couldn't believe it, but he felt as though something was missing and he wasn't fulfilling his potential. He would go to house parties and events, be with big name stars and yet he was drained from doing it. Joel found himself not enjoying it as much as he used to. In interviews, Joel has said that he always had this hunger to do life on his terms and to be a part of something more so he took his own advice and went out on his own. What he learned since he was sixteen he has put into practice and started to build up his own ventures.

Many people thought Joel was crazy giving up a job that paid him a six figure salary so he could feel an inner peace and find his calling. He moved back to Australia and many of his friends thought it was the wrong move to make, but Joel wasn't 100% happy and he wanted to find something that would do that. On contrary to what most successful people do when they quit their job, Joel had absolutely no idea what he was going do with his life. He just knew there was an urgency to quit so he did.

He went back to Australia and because he was talented at sales he did that. There was a company he worked for before he went into the music industry, word got around that he was back in Perth and they called him up. He sold fiber optic connections to corporate and medium sized businesses for a while.

A couple of months later, there was a workshop with the Wolf of Wall Street, Jordan Belfort. Joel had the opportunity of meeting him and it was then that his life changed. Jordan offered invaluable advice to Joel about the next steps to take to change his life around. Jordan asked Joel whether he had goals, it seems foolish to think that such a simple question carried any weight, but it did.

We all think we have goals, to lose weight, exercise more frequently or travel, but what we actually have is a to-do list. Joel discovered that for himself, Jordan told him that what he needed was a vision and not just goal, if he wanted to achieve more than he had to think bigger and in broader terms.

Create a vision and know what you are waking up for. It was there in the discussion that Joel told him that he was interested in self development. Joel decided it was time to create a self development website, he understood a bit about computers and wanted to create a site that showcased important self development articles. It was more of a bookmark site in the initial stages. He later on realized he could make tons of money from it and took pages out of John Chow's and Pete Cashmore's book on how to do that.

Even though Joel's initial response to the site was that he could make money from it, after awhile it became more than just a money maker. It became a place where people can go to for a burst of inspiration and to change their life from the onset. What most people fail to understand is that every successful business didn't start out successful, every idea didn't thread gold at the start. Addicted2Success was no different. Joel had to learn a lot about managing a website and at the start he had no idea how to do it.

Addicted2Success was a bookmark site with videos and articles that Joel took from other sites. He didn't know a lot about SEO or think of his blog as a business, eventually he did and that's when the site evolved into something more than a bookmark site.

Starting a personal development blog is no easy feat, then again starting a business from scratch is difficult whether you have ten years of experience or two. Joel went through the same process, he had to deal with finding a name that was catchy and unique. When he had his site, he wanted to get traction and had to go through the tedious process of getting people to his site. It didn't help that for a year he was the only writer and had to post an article every week regardless of the circumstances. At first Joel was getting about 3000 people on a good day.

Joel was just a beginner blogger, but what made him different from other bloggers who failed to get traction at all was he set up an account on

Twitter. He didn't spread himself too thinly by being on every social media platform. At the time there weren't many inspirational Twitter accounts and Joel took the opportunity to post inspirational quotes from celebrities and then they would retweet it.

After two years Joel was making headway and he was earning $65,000 online so he quit his job that was paying him $55,000. When Joel was in India he decided it was time to write an ebook and he called it the Formula: Secret Ingredients of Online Success. He sold the book online for almost twenty dollars, some days he managed to sell three to four books, other days it was eight. Joel did other things to make sure his site was successful like Adsense, affiliate marketing, consultancy and being a keynote speaker.

Ever since then Joel has risen to the top of his game, Addicted2Success is one of the best personal development sites out there, he also attracts 100 million readers across the world and 50 million unique visitors every month. He has appeared on the cover of Foundr Magazine, Lifestyle Business Magazine and Change Creator Magazine. He is also a contributing author on Success.com and Entrepreneur.com.

There are a lot of reasons why Joel is successful. Even if Joel hadn't have become a music manager at twenty years old, he still would have achieved phenomenal success because of that hunger in him that pushed him to rise to the top. His desperate need to have his own life and not live on terms with what others say or do. Having the freedom to go to where he wants and knowing he can provide for his family and he doesn't have to live paycheck to paycheck.

Amanda Goldman Petri

Market Like A Nerd

"Create your own life." Amanda Goldman Petri

Entrepreneurs have been known to be innovative creatures that are hard to find, but because of the internet we are discovering how it is easier to be an entrepreneur. At the end of the day all you really need to survive as an entrepreneur is an idea and then know how to execute the idea.

This is where Amanda Goldman Petri comes in, she is a marketing coach and created two separate six figure business all before the age of twenty three. That's impressive. She's known as the work smarter and not harder marketing coach. Many people wouldn't have believed that this woman who grew up in a poor part of Baltimore, Maryland would become this successful and establish herself as one of the best online marketing coaches. Her life was tumultuous and filled with many difficult situations that could make anyone go off the rails, but not Amanda. Even her family life offered no comfort, her father was a drug addict and later her mother remarried a man who was abusive. Amanda desperately wanted to leave her life behind, so she dedicated herself to working hard to becoming an Honor student so she couldn't never look back.

However, if you are thinking that this where Amanda's life got better then think again, she got accepted to John Hopkins, it's rated as number fourteen in the world. The summer before she entered, she was run hit by an 80 year old man driving a minivan while she was crossing the street. Her life almost ended before it even begun. It took a while for Amanda to recuperate from the shock and the PTSD that took a hold of life and for years she struggled with it.

Almost dying affects us in different ways, for some it makes them bitter and for others it makes them wonder where their life is headed. For

Amanda it was the latter, she saw that if she died she wouldn't leave a legacy. It took a while for Amanda to figure out what she wanted to do, but she fell in love with marketing on her journey of rediscovering and that's when she started her first business.

She was only twenty-one, even though she built a ton of buzz, in reality it just didn't translate into money. Amanda went back to the drawing board and started her second business, she was a year older and wiser in her decisions. She became a virtual assistant and hired a coach in order for her to figure the best steps to take. Within just a month she hit her first $10,000.

Coaches were interested in watching where this young woman would go next and Mara Glazer approached Amanda and asked whether she would love to become her partner. They founded a joint virtual assistant and social marketing agency. Four months later they were making $150,000, but yet Amanda wasn't content. She was working to the point where she was physically and mentally drained. It wasn't the life she wanted, what Amanda wanted was to expand her paycheck and not her revenue without working to the point of being exhausted. So she left. Sounds crazy right.

If given the chance would you leave your job where you were earning over $100,000 and never look back? For many of us the answer would be no, but Amanda knew that she would rather go out on her own and start up a business where she would work smarter and not harder. It started to become her mantra and the more she looked into it the more she realized long term success is based on working smarter and not harder.

They are many people out there who tell you to work harder to achieve your goals and that results in a massive burnout and unhappiness.

It wasn't impossible for Amanda to start again. Though there were many setbacks she had to deal with. She didn't have any experience in marketing or a degree that could help her with that. What she had were Bachelor Degrees in Russian, Chinese and Writing. She learned technical skills while doing her first business, she learned web design and SEO along the way.

Amanda started her business, many of her first clients came from advertising in paid mastermind groups, mingling on Facebook and on Fiverr.com. Times have changed and Amanda is using automated marketing that takes up less time, but requires huge amounts of capital to set it up. For Amanda her turning point was when she walked away from her joint venture, she started saying no to things that didn't make her happy and said yes to herself. It was when she began working smarter and not harder.

So what made it possible for Amanda to earn all that money in a short period of time.

Did it have anything to do with her Marketing Coach Certificate, Money Coach Certificate or her Law of Attraction Practitioner Certificate? The answer to that is simply no, maybe it helped her, but it wasn't necessary for her to do that or required. She did it because of her love of learning.

So what made her achieve this success before the age of twenty five? We can cross out her coming from a good background, her education or even influencers. What is so inspiring about Amanda is that she went through the ringer, then the gutter and had to walk on burning coal to be where she is.

Most people would have understood if she didn't push forward and would have expected her to submit to her circumstances. After all, she went through a tough break and people expected her to not go far. That's the thing about people they will use your upbringing, circumstances and background against you. Amanda understood she wanted more, she wanted to leave a legacy behind and would push herself past the barriers preventing her from achieving that.

Amanda strove for excellence and that's what happened. It's easy to think that Amanda had it made and knew where to go next, but she had to learn a lot about herself and develop. She came up with a marketing strategy that gave her the results she desired. First, she would do manual prospecting where she would go online create Facebook Groups, establish herself in the marketplace, develop relationships then she would offer products that people were dying to buy.

Ninety percent of her income comes from manual prospecting. Then comes automated marketing, a step that requires huge amounts of capital, but it is more effective than doing it by yourself.

For Amanda it wasn't easy, but she knew what she wanted and that not pursuing it would be the worst mistake of her life so she did. She worked hard for it, then found a sound proof strategy. Known as one of the best young marketing coaches she has proven that giving up on yourself is never a solution and that finding what you love is the greatest gift you can give yourself.

Sol Orwell

Examine.com

"Attention residue is real, and multitasking is the devil when it comes to being highly productive." Sol Orwell

So far you've read a lot of stories of millennials who took it upon themselves to change their circumstances. Sol Orwell is no different, in 2009 he was obese and turned to Reddit for advice on how to lose weight. Eventually, Sol did some soul searching, read a lot of books on nutrition and fitness. He also read Four Hour Body by Tim Ferris, he posted it on Reddit and people enjoyed the information. He then took it from there.

Sol became part of the community and it was then that he met his co-founder, Kurtis Frank. At the time, he was a moderator on fitness on Reddit, they formed a relationship and from there it blossomed into a business partnership. Ideas take time and really good ideas need to first take form before they can change the world. Sol's idea was no different, he had been a redditor for ten years. His life changed when he joined Reddit and the fitness community on there. A lot has changed in the ten years including there being more people involved in the fitness community, when he joined there were only 5000 people. Two years later after he started Examine.com it had grown to 50,000 and in 2016, it was at 6.2M people.

After a while Sol noticed a pattern in the fitness community, members would ask the same questions over and over again. When someone would ask a question, Kurtis would go and research papers so they could give the best answer, but they were frustrated with how many hours they spent doing that. The next day, someone would ask the same question that had already been answered.

Sol found these questions annoying, but he realized that it was hard to find information about supplements online, it took him traveling to South America to actually do something about it. He was visiting friends in Colombia who were postdocs and explained to them how it's hard to find information on supplements on the web. There was Wikipedia, but it wasn't really for professionals and everyone else was selling ads on supplements. It was frustrating.

Often at times we need people who know us better than ourselves to point us in the right direction. Sol's friends did that just that, they called him out and told him he was being a bum and just complaining. They told him to go do something about it. Here was this guy who had changed his life by starting up a fitness community on Reddit, he knew about supplements and what worked and didn't. There was a point in his life where he was obese and he changed his life. What his friends said resonated in him and he decided it was time to do something positive with his life.

An hour later after he spoke to his friends, he messaged Kurtis and presented the idea to him. At the time, Kurtis was finishing his dietetics degree. Sol told him that they could create a website with unbiased, well-researched supplementation information. There would finally be a place where people could get information on supplementation. At first Kurtis resisted, telling Sol that he was busy and was about to start his PhD, but Sol didn't give up the idea and eventually Kurtis jumped on board.

Sol wanted to change his life by losing weight, it was one goal, but by going out there and starting a community, he realized he wanted more. He didn't know what exactly it was, but it was a light bulb moment, all he had to do was listen to his friends telling him to go out and do something. Those words are among the most powerful words in the English Language and in any other language.

It was six years ago that he started Examine. Sol had dabbled in being an entrepreneur in high school, in Canada. He started an online gaming company then he jumped into businesses involved with domain names, daily deals and local search. Though it seems like none of this has any commonality to a company dealing with supplements, it does. Sol always hired independent contractors to help his business grow. In the case of Examine, he hired people with a PhD and experts on public health, lipidology and cardiovascular disease to research on the various supplements.

Three years ago, Sol released Examine's first product which was an ebook called The Supplement Goals Reference Guide. He has sold the product for $49 through a custom site and has generated more than $200,000. The customers loved it, but they thought there was far too much jargon and they couldn't understand it. He brought in an entire team to help him with advice on any topic. In November, 2014, he released a new product called Research Digest aimed at professionals. Subscribers who paid $30 a month, found out twice a month about the latest studies on nutrition.

The road he walked on wasn't an easy one, but along the way he discovered who he wanted to be and sought out to be that person.

Brian D. Evans

Influencive

"Focus on you, not what others think of you." Brian D Evans.

Everyone who knows about being an entrepreneur knows it's not the easiest things to do. Most people see success after the challenges and the uproar, they see the results and not the boulders. Brian's childhood was full of challenges, he struggled to cope in school and had to figure out for himself where he wanted to go next.

Many entrepreneurs go through a period of enlightenment that pushes them on the journey few ever want to travel. In school, Brian barely understood what was going on around him. He felt like a stranger in a distant land and instead of wallowing in self-pity, he went out and did something. Brian bought books to help better understood the subjects and he found mentors. Due to how different he looked at life often he felt like he didn't belong and learned at a young age to stand on his own.

His journey begins at twelve years when he hit his head on a brick wall. He had been riding a pedal bike whilst also playing football at the same time. Most people who have encountered a traumatic event or who have almost died look at life in a different way, they go through a period of enlightenment that shapes them. This is what happened to Brian, he has been quoted saying that this is when he was hit by enlightenment.

He started to question what his purpose was and went to discover it.

A few years later at the age of sixteen going on to seventeen he started his first business on eBay. In his research, he had discovered that many people were looking for parts for cars and he started his business on that. It was only when he was eighteen that he started earning huge amounts of money from it. At the time, the online business was a new idea and it wasn't flooded with people. Competition was rare.

His enthusiasm grew when he realized that he could actually make a living from doing online business. Brian began to learn more about it, he immersed himself in anything related with online business including the psychology of it, how to get traffic and convert people into sales. Brian went on to having several online businesses, selling different products.

The research Brian did when he was first starting helped him understand how to utilize the proper tools online to have a successful business. He studied algorithms, the psychology of trends and different ways to get traffic in order to be different from his competitors.

Though, Brian was considered successful, by many people's standpoint, he was unknown until he was named an INC 500 entrepreneur. It spearheaded his career, people started to know who he was and wanted to collaborate with him and interview him. It became the much needed personal brand for him to push his career to the next level.

Brian continued to go upwards, he became a contributor for leading publications such as INC, Huffington Post and Entrepreneur. Though being featured as an INC 500 entrepreneur helped, Brian has credited much of his success to networking. He studied the best methods and ways to network, he also delved into what people got wrong. In his research he discovered many people hate to be blinded by emails and prefer to be asked or for an introduction. Three years ago, Brian would never have imagined that he would be writing for these huge publications because one of his greatest fears was writing.

What had helped him get over his fear was his short lived acting career that he started six years ago. While he was acting, he would write comedy strips and discovered he had a knack for writing. Eventually, he connected the dots and realized he could connect his writing with business, he then started writing business content.

Influencive started as an idea for Brian to get over his fear of writing. When Influencive started it was based on how to market companies and give solutions to people dealing with their problems. Over the years it has grown into being a source of inspiration and motivation.

For thirteen years Brian has been in the entrepreneur game, time and time again he picked himself. What he has learned along the way, he has realized that he had to adjust his mindset from seeing money as the end-result instead of the journey.

Brandon T. Adams

University of Young Entrepreneurs

"No success story comes without multiple failures. Failure makes you stronger and teaches you things that most people will never understand. The more you fail, the more you will succeed." Brandon T. Adams

If you haven't heard that name before you will. Brandon has many awesome projects that are coming up and he's known as the Crowdfunding King, but life was never like this for him. What sets Brandon apart is he was born in a small town in Idaho that has a population of seven hundred and fifty people.

There's this stigma associated with people who come from small towns that it's harder for them to make it in life compared to those who come from bigger towns. Movies and television shows don't help to eliminate this misconception on what goes around behind the curtains. There's an image ingrained in our minds of people who are super friendly, intrusive, unambitious and who don't have much schooling to back them up in a debate.

Brandon had a speech impairment which didn't make his life any easier and he got bullied like many of the entrepreneurs in this blueprint. What made it worse was Brandon had a speech coach who would come to get him in the middle of a lesson? Those of you who've had a hard time at school because you just couldn't cope know how it feels to be constantly reminded of how different you are. For Brandon, he had enough, he went to his parents and told them that he just didn't want to do it anymore.

At ten years old Brandon knew that he wanted to be a great salesman and he knew in order to do that he would have to be a great speaker. So he practiced relentlessly in front of the mirror. Eventually he became better and in high school his speech impairment had gone. Though, Brandon had achieved what he wanted, it wasn't enough so he practiced speaking in front of his class and volunteered to speak at events.

Brandon would never have thought he would become a keynote speaker or have his own reality show. What his journey has taught him is that it is possible to turn your weakness into a strength. What Brandon did to make sure he got the desired results was he kept telling himself he didn't have a speech impairment. That enabled him to focus on who he was good at instead of the problems he faced. Psychologists call it a self-fulfilling prophecy.

As a kid Brandon got a taste of what it meant to a salesman. His father was an ice picker and would sell frozen water, it was then that he understood the fundamentals of a business and it was possible to sell anything even flying squirrels. Brandon got to learn from his father's successes, failures and up and downs. He enjoyed selling things and he put a lot of his time into boy scouts, fundraising and pop sales.

When Brandon went to Iowa State University, he got involved with the wrong crowd and started getting into trouble. He took drugs, drank too much alcohol and got thrown into jail a couple of times. His grades were slipping and he got a 1.64 G8 GPA. A few days after he was done with the semester, he was thrown out of the dorm and was under academic probation. It was only when Brandon was hanging by a rope that he wanted his life to change, he knew how important college was and wanted to make something for himself.

Come Junior year, he took a pivot. He heard of a man called Cactus Jack Barringer talk, he was in season one of Shark Tank. Jack spoke about how he made millions from his products, lost millions and had to start all over again. Jack also talked about "Think And Grow Rich," by Napoleon Hill and how it's important to change your mindset.

Brandon realized after reading the book, that whatever the mind conceives and believes you can achieve. Hearing Jack talk changed the way Brandon saw himself, he stopped seeing himself as the kid who got a 1.68 GPA and realized if he wanted something bad enough he would get it. He knew he could become a billionaire in his lifetime, all that mattered was believing he could do it.

Brandon was hit with an ingenious idea when he was going into his last year of college. He was delivering ice and he had an idea to keep a beverage colder for longer which he found was harder to do. Putting ice cubes in a normal sized bottle was too much of a hassle and he wanted something different. He came up with the idea Arctic Stick whereby he would put something in his drink to keep it colder for longer and add a flavor. At that time he was thinking of putting in alcohol. He ran with the idea at Iowa State University, won a class competition and graduated in 2012. Now, that he knew the idea was a goldmine, he had to come up a way to get money.

In ten weeks, he had raised ten grand and he started the initial process. Three years later, he learned about marketing, manufacturing and project development while being on a pilot run for a TV show and pitching the idea.

Though he had spent a hundred thousand and three years of his life working on the idea he had learned a lot through that period in his life. Brandon was in it for the money, but because of how determined he was with his dream, he attracted the right kind of people. Along the way he realized it wasn't about the money, but helping people and being a thought leader. Arctic Stick led him into doing a podcast then crowdfunding. In 2015, Brandon's New Year's resolution was to be an influencer for millennials and he started the show in February.

It was a new endeavor for Brandon and there were so many podcasts out there that he wanted to differentiate from his competition so he did a podcast tour. He went to interview people at their offices around America and in eight weeks he made the Top 50 New Business Podcasts on iTunes. Brandon wanted people to see him as an expert in crowdfunding so he knew he had to write a book. For three days he wrote his book on crowdfunding called Keys To The Crowd:Unlocking the Power of Crowdfunding.

To raise the bar he went on TV across America. He would go to Iowa, Vegas, Nevada, Florida, California and Indianapolis and promote crowdfunding campaigns in those cities. He often would find a campaign of IndieGoGo and kickstarter and promote it at the end of the segment.

Brandon promoted so many campaigns people started calling King of Crowdfunding. He ended up doing campaigns for John Dumas and that was a year after he made his New Year's resolution to be the best at crowd funding. He later built a team called the Keys to the Crowd. Brandon raised $453,000 for John Lee Dumas, they made the money in thirty-three days. It became the fifth largest crowd funding campaign in history for a book.

Ever since then Brandon has hit success after success with his projects from Ambitious Adventurer to Keys to the Crowd and Young Entrepreneur Convention. It didn't start that way for him, he had to think strategically about where he wanted to go. What Brandon has proved is no matter how many challenges you have you can always turn them around so they suit you. Turn your negatives in favor of what your dreams are.

Trip Adler

Scribd

"Entrepreneurship is about tackling big problems - often non-obvious problems - that will have a meaningful impact on the world, and this usually involves solving these problems in counterintuitive ways." Trip Adler

Where would we be without Scribd? Imagine for a second if Trip had decided to continue studying Biophysics. It's possible someone would have come up with the idea or they wouldn't have, but regardless of that fact it's indisputable that Scribd has changed people's lives.

Trip Adler like many entrepreneurs had a humble beginning, he was born in the Bay Area, Palo Alto. When he graduated from high school, he went to Harvard to study Biophysics. For three years he immersed himself in his studies, but it was in his senior year that he questioned whether it was the right route to take and he wanted to start his own company. Trip started coming with ideas, he then found a co-founder and went to YCombinator and that's when Scribd was born.

At one point Trip had thought about starting a Biophysics company, but he knew ultimately that he didn't have enough experience to do that. There was an urgency in him starting a company, he wanted it off the ground and didn't want to wait. Trip knew a lot about internet companies so it started there and it evolved into something better.

Though Trip knew he wanted to start an internet company, he didn't know exactly in what. There were so many ideas that were coming up, but that never seemed right. For a year and a half, he came up with one idea after idea the other. One his ideas was to have an online car service like Uber or Lyft. It was like a ridesharing service that was coordinated over phones, but they way ahead of the pack and that time it was hard to pursue the idea. They launched a college classified site at Harvard, unfortunately they couldn't scale it down so they moved on. They tried a bunch of other ideas, then they came across the idea of Scribd.

In order for them to find out if Scribd was a good idea, they put certain components in place. The first one was whether it got early traction, was it going to scale, was it a good business model, would it be a great a opportunity and it did serve the user. Before Scribd, there were no sites that offered subscription services to read unlimited books or written content. The idea was a goldmine, people would pay a subscription fee to read any book or document on any device. But it also offers people the chance to have a social experience whilst reading. They earn money through the subscription fees, they pay the publishers and authors based on the reading activity. What makes Scribd so different from the other book sites out there beside it's pretty and interactive design is that they work with big name brands.

The idea behind Scribd came up when Trip was having a conversation with his dad who's a doctor at Stanford, he was telling Trip that to publish a medical paper it takes about eighteen months. It gave him the idea to create site where people could publish their papers easily. Eventually, they broadened the idea to include publishing any sort of written content and in any format. They built the site, started a community going and through group force found an audience.

Within three days of their launch they became one of the top 2000 websites, this was before people used the app store and Facebook for exposure. They were one of the first companies to grow at a rapid rate in a short span of time. Readers would come and read the materials on the site, upload their material and that would bring more readers, and this became a viral loop. The viral loop continues, they have over 95 million monthly users and 60 million content. It's still growing up to this day.

Trip's goal for Scribd is for it be the largest subscription online library, as of now they have 500,000 books and 60 million written content from the users. They want to make sure that they help authors and publishers get money through the monthly subscription rates.

Jewel Burks

Partpic

"The big thing that I wanted in starting a company is make a difference in my community." Jewel Burks

Jewel has achieved a lot, like many entrepreneurs she has chosen to go big or go home. But unlike many entrepreneurs in this book, she had the backing power of one of the greatest companies in the world. Jewel is a simple Southern girl who got an opportunity to work for Google.

Jewel was born in Nashville, Tennessee, when she went to attend Howard University in D.C. After graduation, she moved to California where she worked for Google. But life in California was relatively difficult and different to being in the South and she missed home. Even though, Jewel was working in enterprise sales at Google, she wanted to relocate. On paper it seems like she had the dream job, Google has been named as one of the best companies to work for, but Jewel wasn't happy. She moved to Atlanta, switched industries and began to work in parts distribution for a large industrial distributor.

She got the idea for the app while she was helping her grandfather find parts for his tractor, the search was frustrating. It was difficult to search online for parts. She wanted to merge technological lens, that she learned from Google and how it can be antiquated when it's linked to technology. Partpic was born.

Burks created Partpic to help her customers help their customers. It's a visual search app that searches for replacement parts. Partpic builds computer-vision technology that can extract features from any parts image. At this point in time they are only focused on the industrial parts such as bolts and screws. The technology can detect from an image what the part is and can also detect its number. Burks licensed the technology to manufacturers and distributors so they can put the app inside their mobile apps and on their websites.

Jewel has been known as the entrepreneur in-residence because she has been doing a full time job at Google whilst she was also starting this business. Burks still worked with Google while she was doing her business. A job on Google now is to help her customers be visible online whether it's their websites or just to enhance their social media presence.

It may seem that Jewel had easy sailing, but working for one of the biggest companies in the world and starting your own business are completely different. Burks was faced with many obstacles. What made Jewel's life a lot different than the other entrepreneurs on this list is she came from a family of entrepreneurs, she may not have gone through the harsh realities of growing up in a poor and rough neighborhood, but she didn't have an easy life either.

Jewel was always reminded of how different she was, her color was brought up numerous times and she watched as their racial identities affected her parents businesses. Growing up, Jewel wasn't a colorblind kid and when she started her business she knew she would be met with challenges. The first being people would question her credentials and would look at her color first.

What made it harder was the other founder was black, he was the smartest guys she knew and wanted to go work for Shazam. It made sense to bring him on the team because eventually she wanted to do Shazam for parts, but it made it a whole lot harder to get noticed.

People often asked her to jump hoops that were too high compared to her competitors, she thought of finding a white male to help her fundraise. Jewel's leadership team is comprised of black people and in the tech world she faced a lot of prejudice because of it, but regardless of all the hoops Jewel had to jump over she managed to come up at the top.

Last year, they raised $1.5 million, met president Obama and Jewel was one of the contenders Forbes 30-Under-30.

Success is determined how much you strive to achieve your dreams and Jewel proved that race can be a detriment, but it doesn't mean that you can't strive for more.

Stacey Ferreira

MySocialCloud

"Start somewhere. Start now." Stacy Ferreira

Can you imagine in a million years someone becoming successful through Twitter unless they are a celebrity? It's hard to swallow. What about a twenty year old owning her own company? Stacey did the unfathomable and she landed a million dollar deal with one Tweet.

When Stacey graduated from high school in 2011, her and her brother decided to start a company called MySocialCloud. The problem was they had no money and needed to find innovative ways to raise the funds so Stacey went to Twitter to find investors. At that time she was a casual user, one of the accounts she followed was Richard Branson. For many entrepreneurs Richard Branson is a rock star without the eyeliner or tight fitting pants.

For many entrepreneurs young and old, Branson is the epitome of success, fame and fortune. He is an entrepreneur who has changed the game for many people. When Ferreira saw his Tweet about inviting people to donate $2000 to his charity, those who did would be invited to a cocktail party in Miami and meet with Branson himself, she jumped on the wagon.

At the time Stacey was a high school graduate and had no idea how she would come up with the money, she sent Branson a Tweet stating she was underage and didn't know how she would attend the cocktail party. Richard Branson responded that as long as she made the donations, he would make sure he met up with her. Her and her brother borrowed money from their father and flew to Miami.

When Ferreira met Branson, she took the opportunity to talk to him about her business plan and her startup. One of Branson's business partners flew to Los Angeles to find additional information about Stacey's internet security business. It only took about under a week for Branson to offer them under $1 million in startup investment capital.

The tactics Stacey used were strategic, she followed accounts of people who she could leverage from and who could benefit her business or infleuncers. Since then she has been a more sophisticated Twitter user and she sees the advantage of maintaining a presence on the platform.

The idea of MySocial Cloud started when Scott Ferreira's computer crashed and it resulted him losing his passwords for all his email log-ins, social accounts and his school related passwords. He had to start from scratch. This is when MySocialCloud was born.

The Ferreira siblings moved to Los Angeles to work with Shiv Prakash, who is also the co-founder and was attending USC. After this that's when she saw the Tweet from Richard Branson and her life changed from that moment.

MySocialCloud worked because not only was it a new model and unlike anything else on the market, they offered a free model and focused on selling it to college students. It was a huge success because people got to test drive it and they had found the right audience. College students manage a lot of accounts.

Stacey's climb to entrepreneurship is different from most, she achieved it at the tender age of twenty and some would assume she had experienced success before. The reality of it is Stacey and Scott had a dream to start a business, they went to LA to be close to their founder, saw a Tweet and responded to it. Found a way to get to Miami and meet-up with Richard Branson. Was luck on her side? The fact is she didn't wait to know everything first hand, she had never started a business before and didn't know anyone famous until she went Miami.

Stacey has achieved success before people twice her age, this brilliant woman is taking the world by storm by proving that impossible only exists in your mind. Her story is a tale told by Hollywood, but it's completely true and she found her way through the chaotic world of social media to do just that.

Stacey newest challenge is building a company called Forrge that helps people find new temporary job opportunities, find affordable insurances, manage their finances and taxes. The purpose of the company is to ensure people live comfortably, have a steady income while not being bogged down by the responsibilities of being independent from any company.

Jared Kleinert

3 Billion Under 30

"Create your own life." Jared Kleinert

Many people will remember Jared from when he released his book "2 Billion Under 20" in 2015. His book titles might feel as though he's referencing money, but in actual fact it is a estimation of how many people there are in that age group.

Jared became an entrepreneur at fifteen years old. What inspired him to pursue an entrepreneurship lifestyle was that the world of normalcy scared him. He grew up in a middle class family, it was a typical family setup, but Jared didn't want that for his life. So at fifteen he started his first company called Now I Get It. Even though he was passionate about the company, it failed. When he was sixteen he started a company called Synergists and it also failed. In the same year he worked for two companies in Silicon Valley, through this experience he learned how to build a company successfully, how to become a better person and to build better relationships.

At Seventeen, he attended the Thief Foundation Summit in New York City and it was here that he came across a revelation. Currently in the world there were 2 billion people under 20. This inspired him to write 2 billion under 20. He met Stacey Ferreira here and together they embarked on a journey to change the world. Three months later, Jared took the first step forward and he pitched his idea to the Facebook group for the summit. Within half an hour of posting it there were 50 likes on the thread and 60 comments. They were also a number of people who wanted to be his co-author on the book.

Jared had the idea, he knew where he wanted to go next, but he also needed to get a lot of things in place. He needed to find an agent, editor and publisher. Two years later he had achieved his goal and he published the book and built a community around it.

Jared accredits his mentors for his success, one being David Hassle who is the founder of 15five. This where Jared worked from sixteen to eighteen years old. According to Forbes David Hassle is known as one of the most connected men you don't know in Silicon Valley. His other mentor was Keith Ferrazzi who wrote Never Eat Alone and who was also the former Deloitte CMO. Keith was Jared's first consulting client for one of his companies called Kleinert Ventures.

2 Billion Under 20: How Millennials Are Breaking Down Age Barriers And Changing The World came out July 28 2015. He co-authored the book with Stacy Ferreira. It sold out on Amazon on the first day and was number one in Business Leadership. Presidential Candidates bought the book and New York Times Best Selling Authors Tweeted about it. Every major publication was talking about the book from Mashable to Techcrunch and Fortune 500.

The book launch changed their lives, it brought with it many opportunities including being featured on major publications, television shows and starting a new business targeted at helping companies understand Millennials better. The company is called Starts With Insight. His new company is still it's early stages.

Going through the gap year experience changed how Jared saw life, he went on to build better relationship, start a lifestyle business, work on his communication skills and to test out the notion that learning can happen outside a classroom. Through this experience he did many things such as posture building, he built different businesses, launched a book and he also learned how to breakdance from a How You Think You Can Dance Finalist.

Jared didn't have easy sailing, he had to face many challenges including his first mentor being a convict who had spent time in prison for security fraud in Wall Street. What Jared learned from this experience is to make sure he finds the right people to guide him through the business world. A lot can be said for Jared, he might have become an entrepreneur at a young age, but failure never stopped him from going hard and choosing his niche. His known as the most connected millennial, he has changed the world by going around the world interviewing seventy-five people who have proved that age is just a number. Jared is doing this again with his second book entitled 3 Billion Under 30.

Nailah Ellis-Brown

Ellis Island Tea

"There's a spirit that the city carries with resilience. There are times when we want to give up and the spirit of resilience that the city carries is what helps me push through. I am not in business." Nailah Ellis-Brown

Nailah had a foolproof plan, she believed she would go to Howard University, graduate and make her fortune on Wall Street like the top guns. Plans never seem to work out because though she did attend Howard University, she became overwhelmed with the student loans she would have to pay back. Her plan wasn't working out so she dropped out of school and went back home to Detroit.

For sometime she lived in her mother's basement, but she had enough of sitting at home and doing nothing. She was tired of living a mediocre lifestyle so she decided to take actionable steps. Growing up she had always loved her family's tea and not many teas had that unique taste so she took her family's recipe. What she wanted to do was to continue the legacy and find a way to break free of the chains that were pulling her down.

The distinct difference between Ellis Tea and it's competitors was in the ingredients, in it were rose hips, hibiscus and peppermint leaves giving it a red color, smoother and fruitier texture.

It's not the only ingredients that make Ellis Tea so different, but it's also in it's origin story. Nailah's great-grandfather came to America from Jamaica in the early 1900s via the federal immigration station on Ellis Island, New York City. He brought with him a family recipe for hibiscus tea. Her great-grandfather made a plea before his death for the tea to be sold and now Nailah's honoring his wishes by producing the tea. She had the idea, but starting out was a bit hard. She borrowed $50 from her mother and went to buy the ingredients, in the early stages she tested batches with her family and friends.

Ellis-Brown went to MSU Extension after a fellow entrepreneur told her about it. She met Matthew Birbeck who is a senior business development specialist from Michigan State University Product Center. He connected her with a food specialist at MSU who then helped her refine her idea and commercialized the formula so it could sell easily.

In the beginning of 2009, Ellis Island Tropical Tea was on the shelves of Avalon International Breads in Midtown.

Since then $400,000 has been invested into the business, the investor remains anonymous. The company has received over $100,000 in revenue. Since then, she has been named one of Forbes 30 Under 30 in the manufacturing industry. Now her beverages are sold in Whole Food Stores and in Meijer across the Midwest.

Though, Ellis has made a name for herself in the manufacturing industry, like everyone she comes across roadblocks. She wanted to sell the tea to Detroit Metropolitan Airport, but they declined because they had a contract with Pepsi to sell their brand. Even her deal with HMSHost and Hudson News that operate rest stops and airport stores, came to a grinding halt.

Ellis hasn't given up though. She has found a loophole in the system. Last year she was awarded the Michigan Black Chamber of Commerce's Sankofa Next Generation Entrepreneur of the Year Award. She decided to connect with Leon Richardson, president and CEO of Southfield-based chemical management company ChemicoMays. Richardson became her mentor and guided her through the process of passing the NSF audit. This would allow her products to be sold into Metro Airport. They will use a clause so that the local products can be sold under Pepsi.

If Ellis had never met Richardson, she wouldn't be where she's today. He helped push her business to the next level and he also funded Ellis Island $15,000 initial order from Meijer. Richardson also built a line of communication with Aramark and Ellis. Aramark is a major distributor of food products to hospitals, schools and businesses.

Ellis has also expanded her business to other States and will continue to make her mark on history.

Gerard Adams

Elite Daily

"We true are the generation that can make history and it starts with us leading the way by not being selfish. The more you empower others...and embrace team and mentoring - I guarantee, you will manifest more opportunity than you can handle." Gerard Adams

Gerard Adams has achieved a lot of things in a short space of time, he's known as the voice for Generation Y. Most people would have thought a college drop out would amount to nothing, but not for Gerard who has a lot of things on his resume. He's a serial entrepreneur, documentary film producer, digital media executive, millennial thought leader and philanthropist.

It wasn't always like this. Gerard went to university like a lot of entrepreneurs, he only stuck around for his first semester before he decided it was time to drop out and so he did. Growing up, Gerard's parents had instilled him the need to go to university, get good grades, graduate and get a good job. It never felt right for Gerard. He saw his parents work endlessly and come back home tired, his father taught him good work ethic, but having a normal job wasn't the path he wanted to take. What he desperately wanted was to be successful so he could take care of his family.

As a kid, his father would encourage Gerard to write down what the stock was, he became interested in the stock market and Wall Street. When he dropped out of college, he started a forum for stock traders that wanted to learn from other traders and investors. Gerard noticed that the forums didn't show any credibility because they had no rating system so he decided he wanted to create one. He created a rating system, similar to eBay, but each member would score points according to how good they were. This was his first initial idea.

This sparked his interest, he became invested in the site, he would sleep at 3am promoting the website. He started with only $1000 and quickly learned about investments, he asked questions non-stopped and learned more. Eventually he got 10,000 people to sign up. In his first year, he got a phone call from a CEO in New Jersey. He was running a nanotechnology company called mPhase Technologies and wanted to advertise with Gerard. He met Ron Durando who was based out of New Jersey. Ron became Gerard's first mentor, he promised to teach him investor relations and offered him a job.

He took up the position of being Director of Investor Relations for his company and in the process of that was building up his own company. Gerard ended up building his company, they were re-inventing the battery. They were creating an infinite shelf-life battery battery known as the nanobattery by separating the electrodes from the electrolytes, which are two separate liquids. They then allowed those liquids to mix with through the nanostructure.

Gerard was also building up the website, writing Ron's press releases and video marketing. This carried on for the whole first year, Ron ended up getting 18,000 shareholders, this is by far the largest shareholder base out of a small cap. After the first year, Gerard came up with an idea to do a live demonstration of the nanobattery, he told Ron his idea. Ron agreed and said he should handle everything. For weeks, Gerard worked on the invitation lists, press releases and managed the PR. Over 100 investment bankers, retailer investors and brokers were in the room. The Chief Scientist Officer went to demonstrate the battery. He hits the button to demonstrate and it doesn't switch on. This was his first experience with failure. He learned so much through it and this was led him to his next company, EliteDaily.

Though he had failed in front of a room of high profile people, they were amazed at this twenty year old kid who brought them into the room. They handed him their business cards. Gerard then started an agency to cater to small cap publicly traded companies and market them. They received over $10 million by the time he was twenty four and he was flying all around meeting great innovative companies then 2008 happened. He had seen it coming and knew he needed another solid plan and the best one that presented itself to him was investing in his own companies. Gerard started doing documentaries on the economy and invested in commodities.

There was an intern working for him at time and he had an idea of creating a website called Elite Wall Street, at the time it was more tailored towards finance. After doing intensive research work, they realized that many websites geared towards to millennials were either college based, humor based or a sports entertainment site. They decided to do a site that covered all kinds of verticals. That was the start of Elite Daily.

Eventually, he sold the website for $50 million. It hadn't been easy at first, but he managed to sell the website. Gerard needed to figure out what was next, he had managed to make Elite Daily global and he had to determine what he's next step was. Gerard met Tony Robbins, he told him that "Success without fulfillment is the ultimate failure." That got Gerard thinking that he loved helping young entrepreneurs, startups, mentoring and sharing his experience. He started branding his story at GerardAdams.com, he then compiled information and content through the name Fownders that he is in the processing of building up.

Ramit Sethi

I Will Teach You To Be Rich

"Anyone can be rich; it's just a question of what rich means to you." Ramit Sethi

Ramit Sethi is known as the financial guru for Generation Y. His site I Will Teach You To Be Rich generates over a million followers every month. He is also one of the richest bloggers so the question here is how did a man born to immigrant parents from India accomplish all this. Growing up, Sethi was opinionated and smart, but he wasn't the smartest kid in the room. He loved cracking codes and understanding how certain things worked.

He wanted desperately to go to college, but his parents couldn't afford it so he devised an organizational strategy to apply for 60 scholarships. His first applications were turned out, he videotaped himself and realized he wasn't smiling enough and he went to interviews smiling. He won more than $200,000 in scholarships and used that money to go to Stanford. His first scholarship was a $2000 award and he used that to invest in stock, he lost half of his money in the process. This taught him that he knew very little about finance and dedicated his time to reading every book on personal finance. The more he learned, the more he understood about the battles young people face with money, he then put together a handbook called I Will Teach You To Be Rich. He gave his friends the handbook and started classes on campus, but few people ever attended them.

Sethi didn't give up and he started a blog. At first, he wrote about credit card debt and Roth IRAS, eventually he changed his stance and realized financial education was a waste of time. At the time he was studying behavioral psychology at school and decided to use persuasive techniques to overcome financial problems. Sethi believes strongly in automation, he suggests people to use automation because people are incapable of making smart decisions on their own. Automatic money flow system is the best way to pay for debts because once your paycheck is deposited into your banking account, it's automatically transferred into your IRA and savings accounts.

He delved deeper into the psychology of finance and his posts grew longer. Thousands of people started going to his blog and writing sprawling accounts of how his advice was changing his life. He appeared on television, publishers came knocking to his door and he published his first book. It debuted above Twilight, Sethi was so overwhelmed, he took a screen capture and posted the best seller list online. He circled Twilight and wrote Dominated.

Though in recent years they have been a number of people who have tried to become financial advisers for Generation Y, Sethi still dominates the market. Like many millennials he uses snark and humor in his writing and that is why people can connect with him.

Sethi is so different from all the other financial gurus online, he doesn't mind mocking his readers and that's why they keep coming to him. Besides that he also doesn't make money the way most bloggers do. Professional bloggers make money in two different ways either through advertisements or by working with companies and sending people to those sites. Sethi makes his money by doing courses, he has a variety of courses, though most of his advice is 98% free. He had a course called Dream Job Elite which was limited to 15 people that costs $12,000. It sold out in less than a week.

He has motivated many young people to quit their jobs and follow their passions by offering them actionable steps to do that. He's not a magician waving his arms around and muttering abracadabra. He advises people on ways to save money so they be financially free to follow their passions. Times have changed and as they do it becomes a lot harder for young people to go up the corporate ladder. The traditional way has failed this generation and that's why Ramit Sethi's voice is building up this generation. In 2014, he launched Zero To Launch, an online course about starting an online business and it has been his biggest launch to date. In 2015, he became generating over 1 million monthly visitors

Ramit has managed to prove anything is possible, do people disagree with his advice, often they do. People who are highly successful will always have critics, but he has proved that financial freedom is closer than you think.

Alexa Von Tobel

LearnVest

"You can't make good decisions, but you don't have to make perfect decisions."
Alexa Von Tobel

Women can learn a lot from Alexa Von Tobel who has become the financial guru for women. She graduated from Harvard in 2006 with a business degree, she realized that her and her peers had no idea how to manage their own money. She read many books on the subject, but couldn't relate or understand the books. Professional financial planners were also too expensive. Alexa also realized that women were not being served well online, their needs were not being met and that's when an idea manifested in her brain.

Alexa worked as a trader at Morgan Stanley for two years then went to Harvard Business School for semester and that's when the idea grew. She wanted to bring personal finance to women in an easy to digest, exciting and unique way. LearnVest went online in 2010, at the time Tobel was on a ski trip with her family. The last two weeks she had spent time putting up content. The unfortunate part was the site crashed because too many people were signing up at the same time. She has built one of the fastest financial planning companies in America. There are a number of tools including tools to visualize a budget. Most of her tools are free, but the financial planner is $299 for a setup fee then $419 per month.

Many people have no idea how many subscribers LearnVest has, but one thing is for sure it has made Tobel's name synonymous with financial success. In four years, she managed to raise $75 million for the company. It may seem that Tobel had a head together from the get go, but it took years for her to build up this momentum.

She didn't have the easiest childhood and that ignited her passion to understand finance. When she was fourteen, her father died suddenly, her mother wasn't sure what steps she should take. When Tobel graduated from university, her mother was taken aback because Tobel couldn't answer basic questions about her finances. Though, after some research, she realized she wasn't the only one and many of her friends and family members didn't know how to manage their own money.

The problem with many financial advisers was that they were chasing big fish and those who weren't part of the wealthy 1% were losing out. She needed to find a way to break ground for those who weren't rich, but need to understand how they could manage their finances better. She started taking notes about personal finance, no matter how nonsensical it appeared to her. She had saved up enough money, had dedicated nine months to LearnVest and was ready to drop out of college. Within six months, she had raised $1 million in seed money.

It didn't take long for the website to gain traction and attention from Silicon Valley. The company was valued at $100 million by 2011 and Forbes, Inc and Business Insider recognized her as being the most prominent female figure in the industry. It took many sleeplessness nights for LearnVest to be where it is today. The recession that occurred in 2007 to 2009 also didn't help, but through working out the kinks Tobel managed to make sure LearnVest didn't wither away like many companies.

Her focus and drive made LearnVest what it is today. If Alexa had given up, she wouldn't be where she is today and LearnVest wouldn't be the ideal place for financial advice for gowomen. One idea cultivated a generation of women who are taking up Tobel's advice and setting themselves up for success.

Erika De La Cruz

Passionista

"Well, there was a dominant belief that I wasn't enough." Erika De La Cruz

When Erika was a kid she wanted to be an actor, presenter or rapper. Her passions didn't change even after high school. She went to college and got the chance to intern at an LA based channel doing red carpet correspondence. This was the chance of a lifetime.

Erika had to spend so much time doing research on the films or television shows premiering on the red carpet, she then had to interview the actors and tell the whole world about it. She enjoyed doing that regardless of how much of her time was spent doing that. For a year she interned for the company and at the same time was attending classes at the college. Eventually, she wanted to do something else and found a internship at a radio station in San Diego. She met great people while she was there including the host of More Music Mornings, Lenny B.

After a few short months, she got to work with him on his morning segment. She kept going to class, but her mind just wasn't there and she would come up with various ideas on content and stories to put out there. Her passion has always been interviewing people. For three years she worked at the broadcast station as a digital and on-air personality and served as the station's marketing director. Erika hated the repetitive responsibilities allocated to her in the marketing department so she started to switch gears and host Fashion Week San Diego. While she was doing that she maintained her media stuff and personality for the station. She also did correspondence on the late show and was re-inspired by all this.

Erika would spend weekends working on ways to add value to the channel and segment ideas. A another impressive event she has hosted is comic-con. At the early start of her career, she was doing YouTube videos then Nintendo and that led her to host comic-con. Most recently, she hosted comic-con in 2015, she interviewed the likes of Quentin Tarantino and Ben Affleck. She also works with the CWI which stands for Connected Women of Influence, the Southern California group helps women pursue their business goals.

She has been featured in Recycle Novelty, under the hashtag Girlboss. It's an online magazine that empowers and encourages women to follow lifestyles that pushes them to chase after their dreams. Three years ago, she presented at a CWI leadership conference and she was one of the eight talkers. She discussed her perspective on business, overcoming and connecting; this was all connected to the unique millennial perspective. In 2015, she went to Sue Talk which is the female equivalent of Tedx and it was there that she was inspired by hearing all these stories of people. That's when the idea of Passionista came from and she decided to do a website about women making headway in different industries.

Erika published a book on it and it's an Amazon best seller. She has achieved so much in a short span of time, she has pushed what society deems possible and become a force to be reckoned with. What Erika has proved is that it doesn't matter how big your dream is, it can be achieved as long as you're dedicated to making it happen.

Many entrepreneurs go through endless obstacles to reach their goals, some don't, but what is evident is that every entrepreneur's journey is different.

Adam D'Angelo

Quora

"Execution was far more important than an idea." Adam D'Angelo

Where would we be without Quora? A site dedicated to answering any question known to man even if they sound like something from a cheesy horror flick. That's the beauty of Quora, no judgment. No people to look at you in a weird way or question whether you were dropped as a baby or you got hit too many times.

So where did Quora come from. The innovative millennial actually was part of the initial Facebook dream team.

Angelo went to the International Olympiad in Informatics in 2002 where he was awarded with a silver medal and is also the runner-up in "Smartest People In Tech." article by Fortune Magazine. Adam and Mark Zuckerberg attended the Phillips Exeter Academy together in the early 2000's and later on he went California Institute of Technology and completed his Bachelors in Computer Science.

The two became fast friends and decided to develop a music suggestion software called Synapse Media Player. It was the first of it's kind and would suggest music according to a person's taste. It became a huge success and was acquired by Microsoft.

When he went to Caltech to pursue his studies, it was there that he created the website BuddyZoo. It allowed users to upload their AIM buddy list and compare it to other users. Angelo put his studies on hold for a semester so he could help Mark during the early stages of Facebook. When he completed his studies, he went to work at Facebook in the engineering department. In 2008, he quit his job at Facebook and went to create Quora. Angelo and Charlie Cheever who was also worked at Facebook started Quora in June 2009.

Quora is so different from many platforms out there, it's authentic and people can expect genuine answers instead of just an information overload. The community also has many big names to it including John Green, Hillary Clinton, Barack Obama, Mark Zuckerberg, Avicii, Jimmy Wales, Ashton Kutcher and Stephen Fry. Quora is similar to Twitter, Wikipedia, Yahoo Answers, Facebook and Answers.com. What sets Quora a part from the other platforms is that real names are mandatory, you have to sign in using Facebook, Google or create a new account. Anyone can follow people, the question or answer and their activity will show up in your feed. Plus, people get a chance to Upvote or Downvote answers.

Adam has built an incredible site and he's still in his twenties which makes his journey even more inspiring. He took an old idea of a Q&A site and revamped it by making sure he would connect to the biggest names in the industry. People who ask questions on writing will get a well executed answer from a New York Times Bestselling author. The same can be said for all the topics on the site. Most of the contributors are the biggest in their field of expertise, executives from start-up companies, tech giants and people from reputable companies.

On the wide web it's comforting knowing that there's a site where all you do is ask a question and a genuine answer will come back to you. The answers are thorough, intelligent, wise, short and precise.

The idea for Quora manifested when Angelo and Cheever were having Chinese Food close to Facebook offices. They were discussing about hidden markets and areas on the internet that had a consumer demand, but there were barely any plausible solutions. They looked at the statistics of Yahoo Answers and found out that it attracts 50 million people in the US. Most of the answers were silly and had no empirical proof to them. They decided to create a site where professionals could impart their wisdom and experience therefore bringing knowledge to people from across the world.

Angelo felt he wanted to leave Facebook because it was time consuming and started developing on the idea, but the company's name started out as being called Alma Networks, named after the street in Palo Alto, California where he lives. They started the hiring process, their first choice was Rebekah Cox who was a top designer at Facebook then they hired Kevin Der, an engineer.

The beta test was done after a few months, they released it to their friends and family through invitations. It was called Quora. The site was getting traction from Silicon Valley, their friends were inviting their friends and the chain continued. By January 2011, they had 500,000 registered users and it continued to grow quickly. Quora only had about 18 employees.

In order to draw more people in they decided to change the website so users could navigate the site easier and find information faster. They also released the app through the Android and iOS store. That same year in 2011, they introduced new features including comment voting, video, threaded comments and credits for asking-to-answer.

The next year, Charlie stepped down and remained as an adviser. Angelo believed so much in Quora, he invested his own $50 million of his own money for the B round of funding the company. They continued to improve and 2013 brought in new features including a blogging platform, full text search of answers and questions on all devices and stats. The stats allow users to see summaries and detailed statistics.

Since then the company has 1.5 million unique visitors a month at a growth rate of 300% across all metrics, it's also home to 16 million answers that cover 400,000 topics. Quora has raised $141 million from its investors and it is valued at $1 billion.

Angelo's entrepreneurship journey is different from most, he helped build one of the best social media companies that changed the way the world sees social media. But in the beginning he was like most of us with an idea, the passion to see it through and the vision of what he wanted it to be like. Angelo could of stayed at Facebook, he was making more money that most people and was comfortable, but he wanted more. He wanted to change the world, revolutionize it and create something so he did. There's a saying, "most won't, I will."

It's that simple, if he had never agreed to start the company with Mark, he would never have played an essential part to the building of Facebook. He also wouldn't have become a billionaire before the age of twenty five and wouldn't have started Quora.

Catherine Cook

My Year Book

"To any entrepreneur: if you want to do it, do it now. If you don't, you're going to regret it." Catherine Cook

Many of the entrepreneurs in this book show us that age is just a number. The saying is so common that people seem to just say it when it regards anything to do with age. The list is endless, but at times thinking of a person who makes it big at sixteen sounds like a strange idea unless they are a Disney kid.

The idea for My Year Book started off as being a hurdle they had to jump over. Catherine and her brother were going to a new school, they were flipping through a yearbook when the idea came to their mind. We all know the pain of having to start over again in a new school, it can be terrifying and what they wanted was to make friends. Catherine was sixteen at the time. They decided to create an online digital version of the year book.

Catherine was fortunate that her oldest brother was a web designer so she convinced him to invest $250,000 into their website. They managed to acquire $4.1 million in funding by 2006 and the site became one of the top websites for kids 12-17. Within 6 years, they had grown their site to 20 million users and 1.2 billion monthly pageviews. A company offered thousands of dollars to buy the site in the early years, but the Cooks had rejected the offer. They wanted to focus on building the website. My Year Book was more than just a digital yearbook it was also a social networking site just for teenagers and crafted by teenagers.

Who can better understand a teenager, but a teenager. They started building the site in Skillman in New Jersey. After that the Cooks merged with Zenhex.com, an ad-supported site where users can post a variety of homemade quizzes. Like every start-up, they hit a couple of walls when they tried to expand. The investors wanted them to comply with certain things that the Cooks didn't agree with. First, they wanted the Cooks to move to New York, but they didn't. They also wanted the ads to appear on the personal profile pages of the users and they didn't agree with that. Even though, the Cooks walked away from potential investors, by 2006 they had raised 4.1 million from First Round Capital and U.S Venture Partners. That same year, they signed a contract with CliffsNotes to provide free study aids to all the members.

The site brought in many features that renovated how social sites should be like. They partnered with a game developer Arkadium to bring flash games on the site. MyYearBook used Lunch money, a virtual currency and people who wanted to play the flash games could only pay for it using this currency. In 2009, the site added the instant messaging client Meebo, in order to provide instant messaging. A year later, they launched Chatter so the users could share media and game, this was to bring members together. In 2011, a Latin social media company agreed to acquire the site for $100 million.

The next year MyYearBook combined with the Quepasa to create Meetme, the new social media site revolutionizing how people meet up. The branding of the website was successful and Catherine Cook still plays a vital role in the management, development and renovation of the company.

At such a young age she achieved success that many would think impossible. She brought together a group of people through an idea that started off as a passion project. Her drive, determination and persistence shows us what is possible, even if the odds are against you, all you need to do is push forward. Most would tell her that she was too young, but age didn't stop Catherine from being a millionaire before she could vote. It didn't stop her from constantly building up the site until it was acquired and she changed it to Meetme.

Sam Sawchuk

Sandwich For A Story

"Strangers are just friends we have never met before." Unknown

Can one person change the world? It's a question that has been asked so many times with numerous answers, but the thing is we normally think of NGO's, celebrities, institutions and charities. What if the power was put in the hands of two college students from Canada?

In the summer of 2013, Evan Beck was visiting Sam Sawchuk in Vancouver. They had this deep-rooted need to help those in need, but they weren't sure how to do that and what made it worse was every idea they came up with was very complicated. They needed to do this in an efficient way that didn't mean them going to organizations full of bureaucracy and jargon. Their idea had to be cost efficient.

They traveled from one place to the other and what caught their attention were the homeless. Many people see the homeless as a nuisance, but not Beck and Sawchuk who were moved by their stories. The homeless all had a unique story to tell, they would talk up to an hour about their life and this was how Sandwich For A Story was born. It was four years ago that Sandwich For A Story was born and since then it has helped thousands of homeless people in twenty six countries rid the stigma that follows them everywhere.

Ambassadors for the company go and speak to the homeless then share their story on the site. Their belief is by sharing these experiences it will shape how people look at the homeless and their voices will be louder. Sam has openly spoken about everyone having a story and it's unfair that they can't share it because of where they come from. That is the purpose of SFS.

Sam's journey all began when he was interning at a tech firm called Ayogo in Vancouver. They built gamified Heart Disease applications, as well as Diabetes apps. Sawchuk had never experienced anything so revolutionizing, but it made him think about how human beings were connected. We were connected when it came to technology, health and business, but on the other side there was a huge disconnect from people in general.

He walked the streets of Vancouver everyday seeing the homeless. People who had nothing and their stories were untold. For four years, SFS visited schools, non-profits and corporations to make sandwiches. Then they would engage with the community and share the stories on the platform. They had the chance to go to ForbesU30, TEDX, UN and CGI to tell their story.

Sam's concept was built up from when he worked at HIRED in Silicon Valley and the co-founders experiences. They were working to provide services to the homeless populations. SFS realized that people with a job had more of a sense of purpose because they knew what they were living for, but the homeless who didn't have much also don't feel like they have a purpose. While talking to the homeless, Sam would be told that they all felt like they had a purpose when they were employed. They felt that they mattered to society and we're making a difference in their own unique way.

They are in the process of using technology to offer a uniquely designed program of services to help homeless populations across Canada.

How it works is that they will engage with existing employers of homeless agencies such as warehousing and construction companies. They will then film the interview using a 360 video camera. The next process is to bring people coping with homelessness in the seminars, helping them to understand the best model to take whether it be one

one-on-one or group sessions. After that, sit them on an interview experience using Google Cardboard.

One of the challenges they are facing is scalability because of the resources they need to bring including the Google Cardboard headsets, so they are looking for ways they can partner with a company who can help them achieve this.

Sandwich For A Story continues to change the perception of the homeless and awaken human beings need for Empathy Through Familiarity. Though SFS has helped many homeless people, it also has changed Sam Sawchuk and made him reevaluate his life.

Jill Donenfeld

The Culinistas

"Give yourself permission to be yourself, play and have fun, be silly. Enjoy life!" Jill Donenfeld

In the world of cooking unless you enjoy watching culinary shows, the only famous chefs most people know about is Jamie Oliver, Gordon Ramsey, Wolfgang Puck, Rachel Ray and Bethenny Frankel. These master chefs have been in the industry for years, they have television shows that have made them more famous and their restaurants are known as the best.

It took many years for them to reach that kind of success people dream about, but what if someone didn't have to climb the ladder like the other greats. What if they didn't even have to create a restaurant, go to culinary school or work in a kitchen. Jill Donenfeld learned to cook by watching her parents cook, her family always sat around the table during dinner and even when she went to college that didn't change.

There was something powerful by eating at the table, a familiarity, spark of creativity and togetherness that oozed out of the conversations. When Jill went to New York, she took that, but it wasn't present in the restaurants. Sure the food was delicious, the restaurants kept popping up, but what was missing was the togetherness. Interpersonal skills simply were forgotten. People are too busy and uninterested with cooking.

Donenfeld created the Culinistas as a way to connect people around a table, to bring the chef and the eaters together. Jill also wanted to connect the chef to the farmer.

This all started naturally. In school Jill would do babysitting, waitressing, writing reviews for TimeOut NY and assisting a caterer. The family where she was babysitting asked her if she could come to cook at the house once a week. Before she finished college, she was cooking for four families because of word of mouth. It was really helping the families and bringing them together so she jumped at the thought.

When she graduated she went to work for Karen DeMasco, the author of "The Craft of Baking: Cakes, Cookies, and Other Sweets with Ideas for Inventing Your Own." and she also wrote reviews for Time Out New York.

Donenfeld had a rural upbringing, when she went to New York city, the myriad of cuisines, busy lifestyle and how difficult it is to start a business inspired to do just that. She took out $5000 from her personal account and made a makeshift office in the back of a hardware store. Even though, she funded the business by herself and didn't really need a business plan, she still wrote up one so she could have a road map.

Though she didn't have money, she found ways to promote her business and promoted through word-of-mouth referrals and she would also email media professionals. Her apprenticeship and stint as a restaurant reviewer helped her build a handful of connections. Jill employs six chefs who work in New York City, three in Los Angeles and four in Chicago.

Jill has high profiled clients including Molly Schoneveld who works in celebrity and lifestyle public relations. Most of her clients are busy working professionals and families. Her past clients include the Kardashians and Gwyneth Paltrow. What makes Jill's business so unique is it offers luxurious services at an affordable price that anyone can afford. It's important that the families can be at home so they can enjoy it.

When Donenfeld started the business she would make house visits, but because of her busy schedule, she no longer does that and is planning on building on catered events company.

Josetth Gordon and Donenfeld co-authored a book called, "Party Like a Culinista: Fresh Recipes, Bold Flavors, and Good Friends." The book gives people advice on how to throw birthday parties for every occasion.

Jill also wrote "Mankafy Sakafo: Delicious Meals From Madagascar," when she was in Madagascar for five months. The book documents her food journey and the recipes she collected in all the regions.

She's not afraid to try out new things, when her clients ask her to cook something, they learn and therefore are constantly improving

Karen Civil

Always Civil Enterprise

"We are now in a day and age where we don't have to have a set job or role...we can create one for ourselves. And we should take advantage of that...because I certainly did." Karen Civil

In recent years, social media has changed how we look at life. It has made us understand the world better, get an inside look into celebrities lifestyles, travel around the world without stepping onto a plane and give people a chance to connect with influential people. Many people have started their business using social media and Karen Civil is no different. She's known as the queen of social media besides Kim Kardashian.

Growing up Karen wanted to be part of the entertainment industry, but she couldn't sing, she didn't have rhythm and wanted to get there by merit. She eventually explored the Video DJ route. She went to work at Diplomat Records and helped several artists with their branding and social media. Karen left the label, worked alongside artists and noticed that many who weren't famous were overlooked especially if they weren't in Source or XXL.

In 2008, she started KarenCivil.com and interviewed many artists including Drake and Nicki Minaj before they were famous. Karen is now known as a media maven, but it took a great deal of work for her to reach this point in her career. She spends most of the day using social media to connect followers, fans and people around the world. Civil uses her YouTube site to give advice, share exclusive content and highlight the latest in pop culture.

Civil uses social media to make money, many brands have taken notice of her because of her influence among millennials. Two years ago, she made over $500 thousand through social media and her website. Civil has made a name for herself by partnering with Carol's Daughter, CoverGirl and serving as social media manager for Beats by Dre.

Karen has been busy, she started her consulting company Always Civil Enterprise and published a book called Be You & Live Civil. She also travels around USA and the world as a motivational speaker. Recently, she was selected to be featured in the upcoming Girl Power Tour which was on April 23 2016, in Birmingham, Alabama. She was featured along with Sabrina Peterson and Toya Wright.

Karen has managed to take something free and turn it into a million dollar business idea, she inspires many young girls and millennials to find their passion and go for it.

Every entrepreneur uses their disadvantages in order for them to stand out in the crowd and Civil had to face a tumultuous childhood in order to do that. She was born in Brooklyn, New York then moved to Elizabeth, New Jersey. The underlying problem was that Karen didn't fit in, she was awkward and couldn't make friends. What made life a lot harder for her was she was Haitian and people saw her in a different light. It was as if she didn't belong anywhere, the black kids saw her as not being black, her and her brother were put in a special class because people assumed English was their second language.

Her brother was super intelligent and could play sports so eventually he went to a different school and Karen had to learn to be comfortable with being by herself. In high school, she still didn't have a lot of friends, but this provided her with the opportunity to discover more about herself. She loved watched HBO's Wire and J.D Williams who played the streetwise character Bodie on the show.

Civil created a fan page for him on Yahoo that garnered thousands of followers and led her to meeting the young actor. This was her first official project and demonstrated that she was good at branding. She then landed an internship at Hot 97's Funkmaster Flex and worked as a tour manager and A&R. for DipSet. She created KarenCivil.com in 2008. When she first started blogging, artists weren't social so the blog was a way of getting out new music and capturing artists working in the studio.

Times have changed though and artists have their own social platforms where they post new music and have SoundCloud pages.

Blogs have had to up their game and change how they approach artists, it's more about content creation and partnering with brands. She has managed to become a successful music blogger by using her platforms to create memorable experiences for companies and she has earned thousands. Karen uses her various social media platforms to generate income for her and to network. They made half a million dollars in 2015, it includes her website and advertising through her social media accounts.

Civil's success is undeniable and because she's now a public figure, people see her in a different way, she's been torn by accusations and memes. She continues to use social media to give advice to people and help them climb the ladders of success.

Ted Nash

Tapdaq

"The difference between who you are and who you want to be is what you do." Ted Nash

The last entrepreneur in this book is Ted Nash, I'm sure you have heard the name before, whether it be on the television or read it in the newspaper. Ted Nash is an impressive entrepreneur and he has earned the name serial entrepreneur over and over again.

Nash has been creating online companies from the time was twelve years old. Since he was far too young, he setup his first online business, under his father's signature. He used his father's signature to sign contracts with he likes of iTunes, ebay and Amazon.

Ted's started making headway when he was sixteen years old and created an app called "Fit or Fugly," the app scientifically analyzed photos to test whether someone was attractive or they weren't.

This in the early stages of the App store and the app was more of a joke, but when people bought their iPhones and tested the App store, the app intrigued them. The app was a huge success, it was downloaded over 6 million times, received 180,000 downloads in one day. Ted priced his app at $1, the App store takes about 30% and he made about $126,000 in one day. Nash was a small town Brit living in a farmhouse in Somerset. For him it was all about experimenting with the App store.

The app was later renamed to FaceRate, Ted didn't stop there though, his next app was called Little Gossip. It was more controversial than Fit or Fugly and an earlier version of Whisper, Secret and Yik Yak. The difference is Little Gossip was intended for schools. He was seventeen when he released the app and the app was just meant for his school.

Nash was useless at socializing and wanted to create an app where his friends could anonymously write about what happened the night before. Though, he had only meant it to be for his school, it quickly spread to other schools, universities and offices. It became flooded with anonymous posts and Nash couldn't handle how popular the app had become.

In the first hour of it being out there, they had about 33,000 hits and then it became 50,000 pieces of gossip. It was too much for him to handle, so he decided not to moderate it and be free-for-all. That's when malicious content started spreading. The problem with the app was that 10% of it was malicious and those who were at the biting end of the remarks became unstable and even suicidal. He started getting legal threats from people at school. Ted started creating buzz with his site, journalists started taking notice. They traveled to his house and would stand outside to talk to him about the site. He was appearing in Newspapers.

Ted shut it down because of the negative press associated with it and the malicious content that kept spreading. Nash could have grown the site and gotten investors if he lived in Silicon Valley. His life changed in a notable way when he licensed Face Rate to News International, he was then offered a position of Head of Digital Product Innovation where he managed and launched digital products for The Times, The Sun and The Sunday Times. A year and a half in that position he created Tapdaq.

He got money from an investment group and at that time the app was called Liquid5, he joined forces with Nick Reffitt and Dom Bracher who became his business partners.

Ted's most notable app is Tapdaq that's an essential marketing tool for mobile developers. It has raised $7 million in funding. Nash has gained worldwide recognition for his app, he has been recognized as one of Forbes 30 Under 30 list. He's internationally recognized and has been featured frequently by various magazines including TechCrunch, Wired and Forbes. He has also been selected as entrepreneur of the month on more than one occasion by BBC and the Guardian.

What makes Tapdaq such a unique app is that it allows cross-promotion, a developer running a shooting game could use Tapdaq to advertise his app to another app. Developers collaborate with each other instead of competing.

Nash has changed since his high school days when he concentrated on creating apps for fun. He wants to help independent developers attract and retain users. Ted has achieved a lot of success, he became the first teenager in the world to achieve 1 million App Store downloads. Tapdaq is also fixing the app economy by ensuring that developers who can't get users because of competition find developers to collaborate with. It's a transparent application.

Ted has changed the app world with his revolutionizing application that helps first time developers meet with fellow developers, and find users.

Don't miss out!

Visit the website below and you can sign up to receive emails whenever vanessa gowora publishes a new book. There's no charge and no obligation.

https://books2read.com/r/B-A-JRCF-OKTP

Connecting independent readers to independent writers.

Also by vanessa gowora

Success Mastery
Your Success Blueprint

Standalone
The Exclusive Millennial Blueprint

Watch for more at https://gowora7.wixsite.com/moversandshakers.

About the Author

Vanessa Gowora is a non fiction author who writes personal development blog posts. A writer by day and a reader by night, she enjoys reading anything she can get her hands on. Growing up many people called her a dreamer because of her fascination with telling events as though it was a Hollywood movie. She has used her story telling skills to immerse herself in her writing and create compelling stories.

Read more at https://gowora7.wixsite.com/moversandshakers.

www.ingramcontent.com/pod-product-compliance
Lightning Source LLC
Chambersburg PA
CBHW020625160726
47991CB00002BA/935